Life, L
Discove
Worth

Christina Kinney

Life, Love, & Discovering Self Worth ©
2023 Christina Kinney

All rights reserved.

Presentation by *BookLeaf Publishing*

Web: www.bookleafpub.com

E-mail: info@bookleafpub.com

ISBN: 9789357442145

First edition 2023

To Myself:

"You are only twenty three years old, and have many more experiences ahead, enjoy life and reach your goals, you can do it!"

To My Family:

Mother - "Thank you for being my rock, my biggest supporter, and always pushing me to pursue my dreams. Relax and enjoy your current years, I've got this!"

Father - "You were the first man I ever loved that loved me equally, and your pride for me always pushes me forward. Don't stress so much, you're the world to me"

Brother and Sister - "I love yous unconditionally! Thank you for always being my best friends, and looking after me"

The Rest of My Loved Ones - "Yous all know how individually special you all are to me! Thank you for contributing to my life and making each day better than the last"

To Loved Ones No Longer With Us:

"To all loved ones who are no longer here, your memory will live on as long as I'm here. Your influence and character will never fade. I will love yous all forever and thank yous for inspiring me in every way"

To Everyone Else:

"To friends, loved ones, and special inspirations, thank you from the bottom of my heart, for giving me friendship, love, and support, it will never go unappreciated"

"To Bookleaf Publishing, thank you for believing in me and giving me an opportunity to start my passion professionally. I will always love and support yous for all you have done for me!"

ACKNOWLEDGEMENT

I would like to acknowledge my own personal passion and commitment to create my own poetry book about my life.

I would mainly however like to acknowledge my family, loved ones, friends, and past relationships, for influencing this book reflecting my life, and (for the special ones) who have provided me with unconditional love, support, and motivation; to reach my potential and share my words with the world.

I would also like to acknowledge, Bookleaf Publishing, who have given me my first professional opportunity, support, and dedication throughout this entire process.

I could not have done any of this without everyone involved, and would like to thank everyone sincerely and deeply!

Overall, I would like to thank the readers, who have provided me with the love and support needed to keep going. Yous are the real superstars.

PREFACE

Throughout my poetry book, many different life experiences, events, and situations occur and are expressed within my writing. I believe each poem to be a representation, influence, or motivation of my own/others lived experiences and concur most of the events did in-fact occur as part of my own reality.

There is a combination of characters, places, ideologies, and personal opinion imbedded within each individual experience, and therefore is true to my own knowledge. Most of the people are based on family, close friends, and lost relationships close to my heart or learning base.

The events touched upon, cover the last twenty three years of my life and I recall best, memories/events which stand out best or have had significant influence throughout my life so far.

My book is intended to entertain, however, mainly to educate, empathise, relate, and bond with my readers through shared experiences and similar emotions. I hope that this can be enjoyed by people of all ages and genders, as it's a general response and perspective on life, trauma, love, and significant events, in which, most of us go through within our lives.

The (Real) Stages of Development

Infancy, sparks innocent energy into new life,
Toddlers, curiously discovering, basic human
function,
Childhood, naivety intertwined with becoming
aware,
Adolescence, emotionally challenged, timely
malfunction,
Adulthood, tricked dreams, responsibility
showered with doubts,
Middle Adulthood, lost in uncertainty
overshadowed with unwilling burn out,
Older Adults, known as Pensioners, reminiscing
in memory and regret.

The stages of life, begin from something so
colossally minuscule,
Each stage, we fight to define our life goals,
believing we are awakened.
Underestimating the higher power, and life
experiences we must go through,
Each stage, began boldly from power that can't
be explained, yet finishes so small and subtle.

Rural Day Fade Away

Back in the day, ma maw wid say,
Oot tae the Monadh, away up the hills 'n' play.
Dinnae get drookit, but dinnae be feart, of
stoatin' roon in a little fearthainn.
Nowadays children, all play inside,
Scared to face weather, brainwashed and proud.
Parents say nothing, we've all gone soft,
Children today don't come home caked in mud.
Back in fur scran, or when street lights come
oot, Just dinnae be boggin maw will gee ye the
boot.
"C'mere you ya eejit, tae a hit ye a skelp,
Howling and bogging, mud aw oor ma stairs".
Today, however, you'll here mums all say,
"Coming up with your dinner, son please pause
your game". Banging and screaming, to get their
own way,
Yet we still obey, thinking it's gonna change.
Away up for a wash, that's gee-in me the boak,
'N' don't come back doon till yer gleamin' wae
soap. Mind use that towel ye huv hud for a
week,
My washing is heaving, n it's cauld this week.
Enjoy your third shower, you've had today,
Children, a stained top, must be thrown away.

And use fresh washing each time you go in, My
washing machine is on one constant spin.
Noo, get tae yer room 'n' dae some homework,
Then intae yer bed, asleep for ten o'clock.
Haud yer weesht, 'n' don't answer me back,
Or, yer da will be in here, gee-in your lugs a
smack.
I'm going to bed, child don't be up late,
I know that you will, but what more can I say.
Try do some homework, or read something new,
I won't tell dad, if you do not too.
Creepin' aboot upstairs ur the weans,
Gonnae no dae that, dad always says.
Back intae bed as the weans know who's boss,
Maw n da have saorsa, fur twenty minutes tops.
Making a racket, keeping the parents awake,
Mum texts the children asking them to behave.
Children get quiet, then five second on,
Begin all again, no respect, just fun.
Am pure done in, ma heid feels like mince, Da n
maw look, 'n' tae bed they glance. Turn
everything aff, 'n' say aw yer prayers, Night is
for sleeping, to be active fur the day.
All toss and turn, nobody at full rest,
All the electronics, putting sleep to the test.
No one says goodnight, or says their wishes or
prayers, A family asleep at night, yet still their
minds downstairs.

Aw the weans ur dreamin', whilst maw n da
coorie away,
The toon is aw in silence, everyone preparing fur
a dreich day. Families ur protective, loving, 'n'
engaged,
Nighttime's very precious, as aw the family is
together again.
Everyone is sleeping, but not extremely well,
Four hours sleep in total, to prepare them for
their day. Families are distant, private, and
rearranged,
Nighttime's the only time enjoyed, as no one is
in the way.
Rural days in Scotland, back in the seventies,
Were times where families were all sharing love,
Times were simpler, and nature adored,
While everyone enjoyed their life, and didn't
always want more.
Rural days in Scotland, now, in the twenty
twenties,
Are times where families divide apart, and chase
up owed pennies. Times are made much harder,
and everyone gets bored,
As everyone is chasing more and nothing is
adored.

Tick Tock Tick Tock

Tick tock, tick tock,
Time races through the clock,
The childhood fades,
Imagination rarely stays.

Tick tock, tick tock,
Teenage-hood speeds up first,
Adulthood is craved,
Not realising these are the days.

Tick tock, tick tock,
Early adulthood springs up,
Dreams and illusions will burst,
Childhood reminders are clung.

Tick tock, tick tock,
Late adulthood in full thrust,
Living for time lost,
Feeling life's just begun.

Tick tock, tick tock,
Old age comes faster than first,
Reminiscent in memories,
Body's unable to respond.

Tick tock, tick tock,
Time races through the clock,
The identity fades,
Remembrance falls astray.

Passive Whirlpool

It begun with a whisper heard lost in the trees,
It begun with a sign over-beaming sky deep,
It begun with a feeling, a shake couldn't release,
It begun with a vision the inner child once seen.

It transpired with a movement,
It transpired with a breath,
It transpired deadly silent,
It transpired living dead.

It sparked quicker than dry-wood, tossed into a
blaze,
It sparked quicker than lighting, after thundery
haze,
It sparked quicker than fire, ignited into mighty
flames.
It happened so quickly, whirl-winding through
craze.

It burnt out much quicker,
It burnt out so slow,
It burnt out the brightness,
It burnt out the shadow.

It revealed beautiful disasters, filled with absent
presence,
It revealed cruelty in kindness, with bittersweet
essence,
It revealed visible darkness, from deliberate
ignorance,
It revealed the loving hatred, in embedded
forgetfulness.

It ended with joyous sorrow,
It ended with chaotic peace,
It ended with melancholy merriment,
It ended with negative growth

Thy Neighbour

Man from first creation, destiny to glorify
salvation,
And starts from hands of helping work,
considers others more of worth.
Sweat glows in all his labour, blood thickens twa
share,
Heart beats wholesome helpings, neighbouring
radiating blessing.
Wealth in lucky measures strikes, as morning
must obey, The magnificence morrow darkens,
silence lays at bay.
Eerie sadness fogs the sky, light shall fade and
slowly die,
He possesses dreams of splendour, burrowing
them into the night.
But he that is unforthcoming o souls deepening
repair, May not face suffer of none, or excessive
ne'er.
Through woes of influence, workings of land,
He shall not suffer, the lonely earth fanned.
He shall not lack the eyes that can see, the food
that can fill,
The ears listening to he, he shall touch senses
that feel very shrill.

He may fulfil greater life needs, many name
credited awa glory, loved, and befriended,
connecting contributorily.
And may creation continuously rotate, purposes
chosen, origins ole man exquisitely embedded to
grow, shall ignite combining twa souls.

Generational Rural Destruction

Rural, is a word, that makes you think of towns,
Countryside's, and rivers, along with trees and
flowers.
Rural life was desired by everyone who seen,
Friendships, support, and love, from a whole
community.

Rural, makes you think, that's a place I'd like to
be,
As everyone who lives there, has a helpful
personality.
Rural towns are magic, and feel special to me,
As everything's exclusive to a small population
quantity.

Rural life, involves, hard work, and liberty,
As everyone works hand in hand, to see the
town thriving.
Rural towns, give you, a unique inside feeling,
As you already know, wherever you go, you'll
be welcomed home with help and glee.

Rural life, has animals, and many fresh
homegrown treats,

With lots of lovely grassy spots, for wildlife to
be.
Rural towns have gardens, with hills behind
their backs,
They offer those who live there, lots of space to
plant.

Rural towns have something, that cities just
don't have,
They are made to look appealing, affordable, no
trap.
Rural life breeds people, who run businesses
from birth,
With so much land, and unity, the place cannot
be touched.

Rural towns however, no longer full of trees,
Flowers and grass non existent, just houses and
shopping trolleys.
Rural life's no longer, where people want to be,
Everyone private and selfish, no such word as
community.

Rural, makes you think, now I want to leave,
As everyone who stays there, is stuck and
struggling.
Rural towns are bare now, with no shops for
clothing needs,

As everything's industrialised, and all in the
cities.

Rural life involves, working hard to leave,
As everyone who has success has moved or
went overseas.
Rural towns will give you, empty promises,
As you will know, or have learned before, they
cannot meet your needs.

Rural life, has house pets, and fresh foods
nowhere to be seen,
With grassy land, bought, and building
overcrowding property.
Rural towns have gardens, and hills behind of
these,
Yet no one seems to see them, or use them
usefully.

Rural towns have lost, the spark we used to see,
They're built for no progression, and no
opportunities.
Rural life builds people, stuck in poverty, no
way of escaping, stuck with old resources.
With no more land, or jobs to work, they're
scraping on their knees.

My Mother Reminds Me

My mother reminds me of sweet floral spicy
wood,
Fruity, plentiful colours, that light up every
room.
She reminds me of musk, power, and strength,
Delicately hardened tasks to match her
personality that never ends.

My mother reminds me of flavour, and high
quality oh so strong,
Embodied with commonality, elegance, and
truth, that help all we become.
She reminds me of comfort, loyalty and warmth,
Yet project's responsibility, dedication, and
moving further on.

My mother is a gentle force, passionately danger
filled,
A presence that can't be forgotten, and without,
the room lays still.
She reminds me of the calm, the storm, and all
between,
A whirlpool of colourful glory, imbedded deep
and dark, unseen.

My mother reminds me of music that talks,
My mother reminds me of the morning sun that rises up.
My mother reminds me of all I aim to be and more,
My mother reminds me of security, comfort, and unconditional love.

My mother is intelligently youthful, the young and the old,
She is the unanswerable answer, the solution to problems unsolved.
My mother reminds me of the plants and trees, forever growing, grounded in place,
She is powerfully weakened, relentlessly unbothered, faceless and full of face.

My mother reminds me of traditions so old,
Family values, that will forever be told.
She reminds me of perfectly imperfect art,
Flourishing while drowning, yet never giving up.

My mother reminds me of everything joyous and sweet,
Embodied with personality, uniqueness, talented and elite.
She reminds me of my family, her glue that is our bond,

A real life angel of darkness, I could not live without.

To Our Father

Thank you for being our hero, and giving us all
pride!
Thank you for always having our backs, and
making sure we thrive,
Thank you for the lessons, and teaching us
everyday,
Thank you for making the word 'father' actually
mean something to me!

Thank you for never giving up, and always
putting us first,
Thank you for the endless memories and
showering us with love,
Thank you for the DIY, we always need you for,
Thank you for the simple things, like showing us
we're worth more!

Thank you for being our father,
Thank you for being our friend,
Thank you for being our supporter,
Thank you for being the best!

Thank you for being everything,
to all of us and more,
Thank you for being the first man we loved,

And the one we now love more.

Thank you to our father,
Thank you to them all,
Thank you for the honour,
Thank you for it all.

I Can Still Remember

I may not be the same, but you remain the same
to me,
I may not look myself, but the changes I don't
see,
I may not hear your voices, and remember who
you are,
I may not speak as I once did, but my voice
remains intact.

I may not like the things now I once adored and
loved,
I may not share your memories, but I still feel
our love,
I may not much resemble the woman I used to
be,
I may not wish, however, to be treated
differently.

I may not express emotions, or be what you
expect of me,
I may not be entertaining, or participate equally,
I may not be irreplaceable, and seem disposable
at best,
I may not be included fairly, as my illness
represents my identity lest.

I may not be the first option, and inconvenient for most I test,

I may not contribute as expected, so I'm pushed out the way instead,

I may not be able to always attend, or have to leave before the end,

I may not be suitable for everything, and this I do know and accept.

I can, however, notice who is really there, as I am still a person in each and every way,

I can still use my eyes, seeing it all unfold galore,

I can still use my ears, but now, hear clearly and take in more,

I can still use my voice, but speak with only trusted friends.

I may be someone different, but some things remain the same,

I may be different looking, but please don't remind me, I no longer visualise the girl you know to see,

I may be hard of hearing and mix up who you are, but I know I hold you dearly and remember how special you are,

I may not sound the same, and say things I never would, but this is who I am now, just give me help and love.

I may like different things now, and hate things I once loved, just go with it, I promise my smile will show it's worth,
I may not have my memories, but share with me again, and know I love you dearly even though it's tough,
I may resemble the opposite of who I used to be, but know that I am happy living the end of my life the way I want it to be.

I may have blank emotions, and seem to feel so numb, but I still feel and know what's real,
I may be dull and boring, but I still enjoy fun, even just in presence, my work is never done,
I may be easily replaceable, but enjoy me while you can and I'm still here,
I may be seen as just an illness, but I'm still a person, treat me fair.

I may be the last option, but I'm first to those that matter most,
I may be such a hindrance, but including me will make my day engrossed,
I may be unreliable and not always show face, but always still invite me, plans easily change,

I may be unsuitable to always have a place, I
already accept this, but know I must say, I am
still my own person, so remember when you
can, treat me as before, no different if you can.

You can however be, the person who is there,
and treats me as an equal with freedom left to
spare,
You can still use your eyes, to clearly read me,
and look between the lines to see what I see,
You can still use your ears, to wisely hear the
secrecy,
You can still use your voice, but now, to
advocate for me.

I am not just an illness.
I am not just what you see.
I am still a full person.
I am still the same me.

Cousin Nick

At Twenty Eight years old we said goodbye to
such a gentle soul,
Taken far too young, he made our family whole.
Although he was taken, before his life had
begun,
He always had memories, best of stuff, and just
as much fun.

Flying with the angels, songs still unsung,
Time and memories we shared, will never be
undone.
You shared with us your free, beautiful spirit,
However we must sadly let your spirit fly free.

Nicholas we will always love you,
Your memory will be sacred and shared.
You blessed us, by being our family,
You had a presence, that remains forever with
us.

Goodbye to our Nicholas,
Family and friend,
Your love and spirits forevermore,
You'll be with each one of us until the end.

Bruised and Broken

Bruised and broken,
Words left unspoken,
Clinging on from fear and pain.
Time moves slower,
Hope grows much further
Together yet alone
Stuck in the black empty space.

Love Sonnet

Thee giveth ultimatums in the name of love,
expecting all thee wanteth?

A chase once did gage upon thee, nay longer
worth triumph

Yet wast 't not thee, who is't did detach, deciding
bonds couldst breaketh

chasing the past, unfixable time did lie, did leave
in emotional harrumph

Love is not rootless, and buds as a flower wilt
needeth, warmth and attention

as sure as clouds, darkness weighs in, but soft
light fades hence

Heart and soul ravined, cunning betrayal and
delation deflection

Suddenly thee're running, shutting 't all down
too lief for expedience

The changeth seemeth to befall as the fusty
season fades hence,

 beauty in discomfort, peace and silence guide
me back.

Acceptance for the love did share, better self
sense

Discovery in heavy thoughts, prospered me
towards mine knack

So, the ultimatum wasn't very much what thee
did doth wanteth?

Or did doth 't just bewray thee dreams by luck
without the hunt ?

Two Year Tangle

We spent our two year anniversary,
Apart on on our own.
We used the time to reflect,
Which made our love grow more.

We've survived a lockdown, arguments, and
snores.
We've battled through the toughest times,
By being each other's oars.

Two souls combined together,
We both show many flaws.
We've managed many upsets, fights, and
slamming doors.

We do belong together, I know this to be true.
We've helped each other through the worst,
And always seem more true.

You'll always be the best thing,
That I have ever had.
A girls who's dreams came true,
She's finally met her match.

I'll love you till forever,

And admire you much more.
As you're the one who joined my life,
And made my heart feel whole.

We spent our two year anniversary,
Apart and on our own.
Yet here we are, a few months forward,
Planning history forevermore.

Fate or Faux Pas Destiny

Brown hair, blue eyes, dimples that, with a smile, subtly rise,
When I think back to the beginning, I remember why we were.
Is it even a wonder how he took me by surprise,
I capture the magic, if only once more, I can only remember why we were.

Thick curly lashes, tight body, and hips to grab on,
When I think back to our intimacy, I remember passion is what we had.
I envision our spark, I grieve for that loving touch, real love can't be found, in each other it was born,
I long for our connection, I blindly ignore both our pain, I remember that special thing we both just knew only we had.

Overgrown hair, sad, tired eyes, frown lines appearing, as lips sadly droop down,
When mesmerisation and fantasies fade, I remember how alone together we had became.
Why do we hide it, pretend it's alright, fight against solving it, until we both drown,

I sit with regret, love, anger, and complaint, I
remember all the ugliness, both throwing blame
and shame.

Overbearing snoring, even breathing I detest, nit
picking each detail, cards dealt off the chest,
Overwhelming emotions, physical trauma,
mentally lost, I remember all the dark clouds,
and deadly storms that arose.
Both reach the realisation that love alone is not
enough, grieving our loss already, although
together still faked our best,
I feel that it's over, I shout that we're done, we
don't want each other, yet scared to dispose.

Faint memories of hairs on thighs of the legs, as
boxers are found in washing of mine,
I foggily think hard to remember good times, yet
bad memories consume me, instantly crashing
into my mind.
Both past resentment, anger, and pain, yet not
full of joy, love, forgiveness, or pine,
I feel peaceful in knowing we have a fresh start,
and wanting you back I no longer find.

Appreciating your beautiful soul, perfect looks,
and knowing your my soulmate, one true love,
and more,

I come to reason, and see both sides, and realise no matter what we can work through it and grow our strength and worth.

Why did we let it go so far? Why are we hurting each other when we love each other more than anyone? Why do we both fix it far too late, and let our emotions ruin our core,

I sit with remorse, understanding, and change, using our last chance for relationship rebirth

Groomed well all over, looking healthy, and recharged, time apart was needed to heal ourselves on our own first,

Both at a mutual understanding, still beautiful disasters at times, yet trying harder than ever before to give ourselves and each other the worst parts of ourselves one hundred percent, along with our best.

One last chance, changing huge parts of ourselves, whilst supporting each other to ensure our relationship lasts times old test,

I feel, think, and picture, hope, dreams, and love, hoping this last time, we can both do what we have to to make it work.

Not the final chapter, but the stage we're at right now, we are experiencing the excitement of the beginning again as we start from the beginning and work our way back up.

Both at the advantage of having a serious history
for reflection, and comfortability in each and
every way.
Yet both being very careful, and handling
conversations slowly more each day, treating
each other equally, respectfully, and built back
up,
I feel grateful, and hopeful, and know we can get
through anything together if we try, we both just
have to heal our wounds, use patience,
remember our love, come together and pray.

When I think of the beginning, our near end, and
this time round, I remember what's important
and can't wait to have our rainbow after the
storm, while we clear the clouds.
Is it even in question, how we falsely fall apart,
yet help each other through, all our"we're
done's, and we can't work this outs".
Is it even in question, that our connection, love,
and bond is real, and how it's so strong, we
became toxic, and bad, instead of using it, to
love each other wildly, happily and loving mad,
is it even a wonder, we both had many a
surprise, we never would've imagined, yet will
use to change it and take everyone by surprise.

I capture the magic, and hold tighter than ever to
our love, memory making, and commitment to

making it work together, causing shock and
uproar.
I no longer choose to remember, the pain,
physical impacts or learning curves that turned
into mistakes, if only once more, able to fix it
we are, moving forward, I'll ensure we only
remember, why we fell in love, and why being
together forever was destined in our first
meeting day, we will both remember, if we use
our love together when times are tough, rather
than letting stress define daily rituals between
us, and destroying each other in every each way
We could be unstoppable, and double powerful,
and double strong, and be one of those "power
couples" everyone envy's, looks ups to, and
secretly wants.

Brown hair, subtle with a little bounce, like
gentle waves rippling in the ocean,
Blue eyes, so deep, full of knowledge and love,
hidden with shadows of undeserved pain.
Dimples that are beginning to form happily
again, as more smiles come out for me again,
Subtly rises the depth of our love, this time
around, with more love, passion, and emotion.

Behind Her Smile

She's the embodiment of her smile,
Wearing it as armour for beauty intoxicated with
pain.
Everyone unintentionally unaware, and
blissfully blind,
For she's the girl they all adore, how could she
bare bloodstained wounds over time?

What's buried soulfully within, silencing the
stories left unsung,
Where emotions surface slowly, before
screaming and spiralling out.
Why such vulnerability, and anxiety, that always
breaks through,
Who am I becoming, exposing my whole
existence as an open book?

Behind her smile she suffers, silently masking it
out,
Vibrantly energetic to others, yet so limp and
lifeless inside,
She puts all her prayers, hopes, and wishes,
towards her healing inwards and out.

Trapped dangerously within her beautifully poor mind,
Unable to escape the darkness, and have peace in her life.
The fear of feeling her own feelings, self doubt starts to set in,
Overwhelmed with emotion, fear of failure weighing me down.

The energy closes darkness around me,
Why is it always so crowded and loud?
Why do I constant relive this?
Why can't the light break me out?

Can it all be blamed on a lifetime of trauma?
Or, is it due to my own shameful behaviours, and mistakes?
I melt down, I break down, I crumble, and fall,
Picking up the pieces, I'm motivated to end it, but put it back off.

As she smiles at herself in the mirror, her armour starts to fall,
She barely recognises, her bare, empty shell.
Where is all her passion, special glow, and love?
Allowing herself to release negative vibes.

I now finally can see, that behind her smile, that girl is me!

I am the girl behind the smile, stronger now,
than I ever could be.

Soul vs Face

Hand to hand we stand, together we can't be
beat,
Face to face we stare, proving the fear can't
defeat me.

Rural life we share, all roaming the same streets,
Community together, fighting against all the
concrete.

Back to back, we protect our own clan,
Side to side, we stay together to finish the plan

Soul to soul, we preach our morals as a whole,
Mind to mind, we educate each other
forevermore.

The land we share together, slowly stripped
away,
Yet we never question, why it all has changed.

Never a minute to,
Look round for change,
Look round to consider,
Look to rearrange.

Arm to arm,
Eyes down the way,
We become strangers,
Yet together we stay.

Hand to hand,
Face to face,
Still together,
But forever astray.

Brightly Darkened

A never ending smile,
Shadowed with truth filled fear and doubt.
An ear that is always open,
Suffocating alone with words that remain
unspoken.

The light in the room,
Surrounded by self-doom.
A sparkle brightly shines,
So deep, so dull, so blue.

May they be the one who will never become?
The one who suffers silently alone and as one.
May they be the ones full of energy, that drains?
The one who believes hiding reality makes it
fade.

A free spirited open flyer,
Caged and closed in their own misfire.
A smile that spreads faster than fire,
Slowly intoxicated mind, smoked out desire.

The spark that ignites others,
Closes darkness is that smothers.
The rare diamond that hides,
Imbedded with pain, trauma intertwined.

Perception

A dark creeping shadow that bursts in to light,
Blinding ice white sparkling oval eyes.
Eyes encapsulated with clear ocean blue,
Defining dark eyebrows, thickly trimmed brand new.

A small athletic figure, stands mighty and bold,
Strength hidden in tight muscles, and hips you can hold.
Body full of beauty, stories, self love and care,
One look, one touch, you're already dangerously obsessed.

Skin softer than a newborn, matured as fine as wine,
Sallow toned, trim and structured bones, kept well and fine.
Lips small, yet so plump, tones of rose, glossy and bright,
Soft and comforting, smiling, hiding days of pain and heavy rain.

Dark fluffy hair, thick with slight, subtle curls,
Lighter strokes shine the light, as the hat that hides it is placed upon.

Stylish clothes paired thoughtfully, simple,
trendy, and stated,
Tightly hugging the definition, in all the right
ways and places.

Surprisingly unfazed, as vibes radiate colourful
purity,
Sensing freedom, memories, and love, instant
mutual security.
Connections fast, overloaded emotions, instantly
locked together,
Indescribable perfection, imperfectly bonded in
tether.

Optimism

Each goodbye means a new hello,
Each new experience, allows bad habits to die.
Each lost friend opens space for one truer,
Each bad day leaves room for improvement.

Each season means room for a change,
Each creature acts different when life's
rearranged.
Each cloud surely follows with sunshine,
Each bad thought is drowned out with positive
vibes.

Each faced fear proves limits are endless,
Each new opportunity presents the unknown.
Each milestone lost, motivates us to move fast,
Each curveball we take, is an experience not
missed but made.

Each negative thought, event, or real pain, can
be turned around positively swayed,
Each life ending trauma, never overcame, can be
used as power, strength and self gain.
Each big or small problem, slowly will fade, as
every events works in opposite ways,

Each dark, or bad day, must always come to bay,
and greater lies always after the wait.

Milton Keynes UK
Ingram Content Group UK Ltd.
UKHW020644091023
430221UK00015B/675